This little light of mine

When the love comes trickalin' down

10

Down by the riverside

* like a plucked double bass.

14

The new *Faber Young Voices* series is devised specifically to address the needs of young or newly-formed choirs looking for easy, yet rewarding new repertoire.

Each volume offers:

- A coherent group of pieces to help with concert planning

- Arrangements or original pieces for soprano and alto voices with a manageable piano accompaniment

- An *optional* third line with a narrow range for 'baritone' (newly-broken or unstable voices) or low alto

- Excellent value for money

  The series aims to span the fullest possible range of repertoire - both traditional and popular new material from folksongs, spirituals and calypsos to show songs and Christmas favourites.

- Faber Young Voices – the choral series for young choirs!

Also from Faber Music: *Faber Choral Programme Series*

This highly-acclaimed repertoire series for both mixed- and upper-voice choirs offers a wealth of fresh material from the 18th, 19th and 20th centuries in new editions representing superb value for money.

Currently includes works by Purcell, Schubert, Schumann, Mendelssohn, Bruckner, Dvořák, Verdi, Debussy, Fauré, Saint-Saëns, Stanford, Parry, Holst, Bridge, Warlock, Gilbert & Sullivan, Britten and Vaughan Williams, as well as arrangements of folksongs and show tune hits. For further details contact your local music shop, or Faber Music at the address below.

ISBN 0-571-51523-1

Faber Music · 3 Queen Square · London

Music drawn by Christopher Hinkins / Cover design by S & M Tucker / Printed in England by Caligraving Ltd

9 780571 515233

YEAR 2
READING
National Curriculum Tests

Guidance and mark schemes

■■ SCHOLASTIC

Scholastic Education, an imprint of Scholastic Ltd
Book End, Range Road, Witney, Oxfordshire, OX29 0YD
Registered office: Westfield Road, Southam,
Warwickshire CV47 0RA

www.scholastic.co.uk

© 2016 Scholastic Ltd

23456789 789012345

A British Library Cataloguing-in-Publication Data
A catalogue record for this book is available from the
British Library.

ISBN 978-1407-15911-9

Printed and bound in China by Hung Hing Offset Printing

Author
Graham Fletcher

Series consultants
Lesley and Graham Fletcher

Editorial team
Rachel Morgan, Tracey Cowell, Anna Hall,
Helen Lewis, Shelley Welsh and Jane Jackson

Design team
Nicolle Thomas and Oxford Designers and Illustrators

Paper 1 Acknowledgements
Illustrations: Moreno Chiacchiera, Beehive Illustration
Photographs: Test B, Paper 1: © Fotogenix/Shutterstock.com; © Yorkman/Shutterstock.
com; © Matej Kastelic/Shutterstock.com; © Andrew Roland/Shutterstock.com. Test
C, Paper 1: © Zebra0209/Shutterstock.com; © Elmm/shutterstock.com; © Kjersti
Joergensen/Shutterstock.com; © Sergey Bogomyako/Shutterstock.com; © Rob Kints/
Shutterstock.com; © Anadman Bvba/Shutterstock.com; © Varuna/Shutterstock.com; ©
Nejron Photo/Shutterstock.com
Text: The publishers gratefully acknowledge permission to reproduce the following
copyright material:
Test A, Paper 1: Scoular Anderson c/o Caroline Sheldon Literary Agency Ltd. for the use
of an extract from 'Backseat's Special Day' by Scoular Anderson. Text © 1996, Scoular
Anderson; Graham Fletcher for the use of 'How to write a party invitation'. Text © 2015,
Graham Fletcher.
Test B, Paper 1: Holroyde Cartey Literary Agency for use of extracts and images from
The Snow Lambs by Debi Gliori; Graham Fletcher for the use of 'Floods'. Text © 2015,
Graham Fletcher.
Test C, Paper 1: Graham Fletcher for the use of 'Norway' and 'Trolls'. Text © 2015,
Graham Fletcher.

Acknowledgements
Extracts from Department for Education website
© Crown Copyright. Reproduced under the terms
of the Open Government Licence (OGL). www.
nationalarchives.gov.uk/doc/open-government-
licence/version/2/

Every effort has been made to trace copyright
holders for the works reproduced in this publication,
and the publishers apologise for any inadvertent
omissions.